Phonics Tales!

The Trolls Take a Trip

by Maria Fleming
illustrated by Doug Jones

SCHOLASTIC INC.

New York • Toronto • London • Auckland • Sydney
Mexico City • New Delhi • Hong Kong • Buenos Aires

Designed by Maria Lilja
ISBN-13: 978-0-439-88471-6 • ISBN-10: 0-439-88471-3
Copyright © 2006 by Scholastic Inc.
All rights reserved. Printed in the U.S.A.

First printing, December 2006

12 11 10 9 8 7 6 5 4 3 2 1   6 7 8 9 10 11/0

Phonics Fact

Tr is a blend. Blends are two consonants whose sounds are blended together when you say them. You can hear the *tr* blend at the beginning of **trolls**, **tradition**, **trip**, and **trout**. What other *tr* words can you find in this story? Look at the pictures, too!

The **trolls** have a **tradition**. Every summer, they make a **trip** to Lake **Trout**.

The **trolls travel** to Lake **Trout** from near and far.

They **travel** by **truck** and **trailer**.

They **travel** by **train** and by **trolley**. Some **trolls** even **travel** by **tractor**!

The **trolls** bring **trays** of **treats**. They have a picnic under the **trees**.

The **trolls** fish in Lake **Trout**.

The **trolls** play games and **try** to win **trophies**.

Their favorite game is racing **tricycles** around a **track**.

At night, the **trolls** play **trumpets** and **trombones**.

The **trolls** sing and dance. They have **tremendous** fun.

At the end of the **trip**, the **trolls** get back
into their **trucks** and **trailers**.

They get back onto the **trains**, **trolleys**, and **tractors**.

Then the **trolls travel** home with memories to **treasure**. They would not **trade** their **tradition** for anything—not even a **trillion** dollars!

TR Riddles

Listen to the riddles. Then match each riddle with the right *tr* word from the box.

Word Box

trip	treat	train	tree	trumpet
tractor	trout	trolley	trophy	tray

1 This is something tall that grows.

2 You find this vehicle on a farm.

3 It rhymes with *jolly*.

4 This is a kind of fish.

5 You play music on this.

6 It is something tasty to eat.

7 This moves along tracks.

8 This is flat and you carry things on it.

9 It rhymes with *rip*.

10 This is a kind of prize.

TR Cheer

Hooray for *t-r*, the best sound around!

Let's holler *t-r* words all over town!

There's **troll** and **trip** and **tree** and **true**.

There's **truck** and **train** and **treasure**, too!

There's **track** and **treat** and **trash** and **tray**.

There's **trot** and **trick** and **trap**—hooray!

T-r, *t-r*, give a great cheer,

For the most **tremendous** sound you ever will hear!

Make a list of other *tr* words. Then use them in your cheer.